SMART

Presenter

Stand and Deliver (sans PPT)

Bharath Gopalan

presents

SMART *Presenter*

Stand and Deliver (sans PPT)

Bharath Gopalan

Also by the Author:

Break Your Boundaries (2014)

ISBN-13: 978-1530050215
ISBN-10: 1530050219

~ Opening Note ~

How does a sculptor turn an ordinary stone into a beautiful statue? All he does is to chisel away the superfluous material to cull out the beauty that is already in it. It is quite apparent that he cannot sculpt a statue merely with his hands and he needs the help of a versatile toolkit with a wide range of tools to work on different elements. It is the ability in picking the right tools and using them dexterously that can turn a stone into a statue. Skills and tools go together. Master craftsman gains dexterity as he becomes more and more adept at the use of his tools.

Tools for Professional Excellence

The same is true with professional excellence too. We all constantly strive to develop our skills and pursue excellence in whatever we do. Like the sculptor uses his tools, we use the tools - tools of mind – that help us to chisel away the ineffective behaviors and shape the right behaviors. All the excellence is already in you and all that you need is to discover it and bring it out by using the right tools of mind.

The intention of SMART *Presenter* is to provide you with a set of *Smart Tools* that can help you in emerging as a competent and confident presenter. These tools are simple to use and easy to remember. They provide you with an overall framework for designing and delivering your presentations in an impactful manner. In the opening chapter of the book, you will know how these *Smart Tools* have come about and why you will find them very handy in accessing and applying them to your life situations.

Discovery Learning

Before you go, let me share about a particular style with which the *Smart Tools* are introduced in most chapters of this book.

I learnt this style of introducing new concepts from one Professor Tikekar, who taught Operations Research at IISc, Bangalore. Whenever he taught something new – a new concept or a method - he would go on as though we knew it already and start straight away illustrate it with some example without giving the background details. He would then ask us to make guesses and ask questions to find out what was coming, and then would go about explaining the underlying theory. This kind of *'discovery learning'* worked very well not only in remembering them for long, but reinforcing the understanding of the concept, as well as the application of the tool.

This book has been styled in a similar fashion: The chapters will start with a *'Demo'* of the *Smart Tool* that is being dealt in the chapter. Before you are introduced to the tool, you will be asked to guess and *'Discover'* the Tool for yourself. This is followed by the *'Description'* of the tool and the key points to keep in mind while applying this tool. At the end of the chapter, you will find a *Checklist* to quickly summarize the key points of the tool. A workbook has been appended towards the end to serve as a *DIY* (do it yourself) kit.

In essence, the process used in this book goes thus:

Demo → Discovery → Details → DIY (do it yourself)

I am sure you will find this process useful, since I have seen using the same model in my training workshops and my participants have always found this approach very practical in helping them take the learning to the field.

Surprise yourself

Treat this book like a workshop and go about trying the exercises in your context. You will be surprising yourself not with new ways of doing things, but building those skill-sets the book intends to help you with.

It is also possible that your guess could turn out to be better than the term used in the book, in which case you can help evolve the tool by sharing it with me. Let's talk about it more when we come to the end of the book.

Bharath Gopalan

~Dedicated to my beloved mother ~

Icons used in the Book

Demo → Discovery → Description → DIY

Demo	You will come across an illustration or example that will serve as the 'demo' for the application of the Tool.
Discovery	From the Demo, you will discover the *Smart Tool* for yourself by guessing expansion of the acronym SMART – the trigger words to remember the *Smart Tool*
Description	You will find here the description of the *Smart Tool* and how to use it in your specific context
DIY	A Workbook is appended at the end of the book which provides you with 'DIY' sheets for hands-on use of the tool.
Checklist	A checklist is provided at the end of each chapter for a quick glimpse on the application of the *Smart Tool* discussed in the chapter.

~ Contents ~

Introducing S.M.A.R.T Tools

What are Mind Tools?

We all have had some experience of using a physical tool. For instance, a hammer helps us to drive a nail into the wall by converging the force we apply to a single point. Like the physical tools serve as extension of human body that enable us do things that cannot be done otherwise, the 'mind tools' expand our mental abilities and facilitate effective use of our mental processes. There are many mind tools which we may be using without even realising we are using one. For instance, the *Things-To-Do list* is a simple mind tool that helps us remember and prioritise our schedule for the day. *Brainstorming* is a mind tool that triggers generation of divergent and creative ideas on a specific theme. *Fishbone diagram* is a mind tool that helps mapping and classifying the causes for a particular problem. Edward De Bono's "*Six Thinking Hats*" and Tony Buzan's '*Mind Mapping*' are some of the well-known mind tools.

Why Hooks for Mind Tools?

We all have come across a good number of useful techniques or mind tools for every imaginable situation in our life time. But we may not be putting them to regular use. Reason: we are not able to immediately access them from our memory as and when we need. For instance, we have come across useful tips and tools for delivering an impactful presentation, or staying assertive and saying an emphatic 'no'. But when we need them in real life situations, we hardly are able to ferret out instantly from our mental attic and put them to use.

How do we activate our mind to access those techniques that we already know so that we can do whatever we are doing better. It calls for installing some kind of search engine in our brain that could google and throw up the items we want with the help of some key words.

Acronym as memory hooks

We remember with gratitude those teachers who made learning fun or, who taught us some easier ways for remembering things. I remember a particular chemistry teacher for the crazy phrase he gave us: 'LeO says GeR'. This helped me a great deal in clearing the confusion between oxidation and reduction. Though these concepts have nothing to do with my life or my job for the last thirty years, I still do remember what he taught me, thanks to the acronym LeO and GeR: Loss of electrons is Oxidation (LeO) and Gain of electrons is Reduction (GeR).

Use of acronyms is one effective way for registering things in our memory. The alphabets of the acronym serve like hooks on which the words connected to them are hung. The moment you get the acronym, the related words pop out as though they were hanging on the hooks.

Mind-Tools go SMART

Elegant & Efficient: There is something very appealing about the word 'smart'. Smart work does not only mean a very efficient and elegant way of working, but it also represents an acronym which is very popular among management practitioners. Who has not heard of the **S.M.A.R.T.** criteria for goal-setting - **specific, measurable, achievable, realistic and time bound.**

Magic five: The word SMART is made of five alphabets and the number five is countable with fingers of one hand and hence, when it comes to remembering, five items or five steps can easily be remembered by human mind without much efforts. The number of items an average person can hold in working memory, referred to as 'memory span', is found to be between 5 and 9, as suggested by the oft-cited experiments by George Miller in 1956. (Source: http://www.human-memory.net)

Wonder Acronym: Look at the word SMART- the five alphabets it is composed of. It is fascinating to see that these five letters are among the top seven letters that form the beginning of most words in English (Wikipedia: The first letter of an English word, from most to least common, s a̲ c m̲ p r̲ t̲ b f g d l h i e n o w u v j k q y z x). Around 35 to 40 percent of the words in English have one of the five letters of SMART as their initial letters. That also makes SMART a wonder acronym.

Smart is such a mesmerising word that is has been used in the most ancient times with similar meaning. Two of the most ancient languages use very-similar sounding words to mean smartness: *samartha* (समर्थ) in sanskrit meaning *'strong or powerful, competent, capable of'* and ***samarthyan*** (சாமர்த்தியன்), in Tamil meaning *'a competent, skilful person'*.

Enamoured by the word 'Smart', I started smarting, un-smarting and re-smarting various tools and techniques for use in my training sessions. And the culmination of this smart saga is this book. All the Mind Tools you will come across in this book use the acronym S.M.A.R.T. and hence they are deservedly called as **'Smart Tools'**.

Force-fit or Flowing free?

On the first read, if you find any specific tool has been force-fit into the acronym, the best way to check that is to put it to test by using it in a real-life situation. It is only by the application of the tool, you can know whether it works. 'I hear, I forget; I see, I remember; I do, I understand.' So, experiencing the tool not only leads to understanding its usage, but in recalling it effortlessly from your memory.

When you apply the tool, are you at ease in action? Are you free-flowing with the tool helping you prompt the sequence of actions? Do you find yourself more effective? Then, it is working. Or better still, if it triggers certain thoughts and actions that can refine it further, then that will help you in internalising the tool and making it a part of you.

Smart ways to use *Smart Tools*

- **Structure:** Smart Tools provide you with a structure or framework for developing your course of action. The tool may be just a tentative checklist or a gist of some relevant concepts or a series of steps to doing something.

- **Memory:** What we store in our memory space is useful only when we are able to access it quickly at the time of need. The acronym SMART serves as a Mnemonic to recall the tool you need.

- **Approach:** Smart Tools provide you with an Approach - a list of things to do or sequence in which to be done.

- **Recipe:** Smart Tools are like Recipe that can be tried, tested, tasted and improved upon. They serve as a simple base on which you can build and refine your actions to suit your situation

- **Tips:** It's about getting it right and getting it readily. Tools are just the Tips or pointers you need for taking quick action without getting into endless analysis.

SMART PRESENTER

1. Presenter's Dilemma

You receive a phone call and the caller says that she is calling from an organisation called *Be The Change* and wants you to be the key speaker for their annual event falling next month. They would like you to be a speaker since you are an accomplished professional and your story, they believe, would trigger people to take charge of initiating change in their lives.

What would be your immediate reaction? It is not what response you give the caller, but think about what thoughts would occur in you - how you would react within yourself? Here's a range of possible reactions; Rate your reaction on a scale of 1 to 10 and encircle the number closer to what you feel.

10. **Yes, I will do it**

9. I can do it

8. **Hope I can do it!**

7.   I think I can take up

6.   I will probably do it

5.   I will try to do it

4.   I want to do it, but you know…

3.   You really want me to do it?

2.   I don't think I can do it

1.   **No, I will never do it in my life**

Way To Go

- If your reaction is anywhere in the range of 2 and 8, then you are in the right place. If your reaction ranges from strong self doubt (2) to slight hesitation (8), you will find the following chapters of certain help. If you get a hang of the tools in this book, then you will most probably be giving a resounding 'Yes, I will do it' when the next opportunity is around. If there is no opportunity coming up, you will be tempted to create opportunities to get on to stage and deliver your talk.

- If your reaction is 9 or 10, you must really be a great learner to be reading this book.

- If it is 1, then you may be the better person to judge as to why you are reading this.

At the Root of the Dilemma

'To do it or, not to do' is a dilemma you come across when

faced with a situation demanding you to do something new-something for the first time. You want to do it, but you are not sure whether you will be able to do it. It applies not only to 'public speaking', but to anything that calls for taking emotional or physical risk. When I went on a holiday to a hill valley, I was asked to try 'paragliding'. While I was tempted by the joy of flying, I was deterred by the fear of falling, which was assuaged by the coach who taught me the skills.

While your interest pushes you to do it, your self-doubt pulls you back strongly. If we understand what is at the root of your nervousness to do anything, then it is easy to handle it. At the root of lack of confidence is the lack of skills. Only way to overcome this nervousness arising out of 'lack of skill' is to put in a systematic preparation and follow it with rigorous practice.

Great presenters ooze confidence and speak effortlessly. They are adept at the art of engaging people's hearts and minds and moving their audience to action. While we do get to see the presenter's magic on the stage, what we miss to see is the hours and hours of efforts that they put into meticulous planning and rigorous preparation.

The ability to deliver exceptional talks can be developed if you adopt a methodical approach and put in a systematic practice. The following chapters will provide you with a set of nine tools that will give you a very structured framework for preparing and delivering powerful presentations.

The following chapters will cover all the stages of your presentation right from the word go to delivering it on the d-day.

1. Gather the First Facts First
2. Do Your Groundwork
3. Design and Develop Your Talk
   - o Opening
   - o Mainframe
   - o Closing
4. Adorn Your Talk to Reinforce Your Ideas
5. Rehearse & Deliver

2. Grab Their Attention

18 Minute Rule

"No talk can exceed 18 minutes in length" is a strict rule for the speakers of TED talks. You may wonder why this 18 minute rule? TED Curator Chris Anderson says 18 minutes is long enough to be serious and short enough to hold people's attention.

Studies suggest that an effective speaker can hold the attention of audience for about 20 to 30 minutes at a stretch. Why go to research, for that matter, have we not experienced it ourselves? Not to talk of the dragging lectures and boring presentations, even the interesting talks would hardly be able to hold us beyond 15 to 20 minutes at

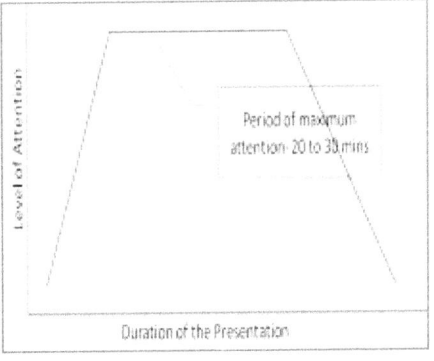

one go. Next time, when you are listening to a talk, just get present to the number of times your attention drifts away from the talk. Hence, as a presenter, it is vital for you to pack the contents of your talk in such a way that you not only get your audience quickly interested in the topic, but also have their rapt attention for at least the next 15 to 20 minutes. It would be ideal to set a 20 minute cap for presentation with flexibility to extend at the most by 10 minutes to handle the post-talk discussions.

However, there are situations and subjects where the talk cannot fit into tight time slots of twenty or thirty minutes. Some subject matters may demand longer sessions of say an hour or two. In such cases, it is a good idea to intersperse the talks with soft breaks rather than delivering it at one go all the way. Soft-breaks help you break the monologue by engaging the audience in some discussion time or a group activity. Otherwise the monotony of listening will fatigue the audience and holding the attention will be a challenge even if they are really keen on the topic. So involving them in some contextual discussion or activity will trigger them into thinking and gather their attention back to the subject.

Anyway, there are more primary questions and concerns about the decision itself- when and how do you decide to commit for a presentation? what facts and details should you get at the point of making this decision? Let's begin at the beginning.

3. First Facts First

Joe, a HR manager, was invited to deliver a talk to an out-going batch of b-school students. Joe himself was a student of that college some eight years back and now that he has progressed fairly well in his career, his college wanted to showcase him to the current batch of students which by itself will be a motivation. He also relished this idea and instantly said 'yes' to be a speaker in the college event. Before he agreed, he asked a few quick questions like what subject he was expected to speak on, when the event had been scheduled and who the other speakers were. As he sat down with his laptop to think up his talk, he felt he was stuck. He didn't have enough information to work his way through the talk. What more information would you have gathered, if you were asked to give the talk?

Let's look at a few things, the first facts, that you must gather and ascertain before you say 'yes' to a request for 'speaking' or call for a presentation. These are details you need to necessarily ask before confirming your acceptance.

As you go through the demo of the *Smart Tool* for gathering the 'first facts, go about guessing the words with the help of the first letter and the dashes indicating the number of letters. This tool is discussed in the later part of the chapter

Demo

S _ _ _ _ _ _

These are the first questions Joe should probably be asking: "What would you expect me to speak on? If you want me to choose the subject, let me know what would be of interest to this group of participants? What is the theme of the event?"

M_ _ _ _ _ _

As a speaker, this is something Joe has to decide for himself. Once they spell out the area or subject matter, on which they expect him to talk, he will instantly know whether he can handle it or not.

Your confidence to take up a talk will depend on the level of expertise you have on the subject matter. If you are allowed to choose the topic by yourself, you will naturally choose a subject over which you have a reasonable mastery which comes from the kind of studies or work you have done in the area.

A_ _ _ _ _ _ _

The next questions that Joe would be interested in are:

- Who are going to be attending this talk?

- How many are going to be there? What is the expected

size?

- Why are they interested in this specific subject?

R__ __ __ __ __ __ __

The next questions will relate to:

- Where is the event going to be held? Is it in open auditorium or closed hall?

- Will I have to speak from a fixed lectern and mike? Can I move around the dais as I speak? If so, do you have a collar mike or a handheld mike?

- What possible presentation aids can be used- PowerPoint, flipcharts, video films etc?

- Will the event be video-graphed or recorded?

T__ __ __ - S __ __ __

- When is the event scheduled?
- What is the slot for me? What is the duration for my talk?
- What are on the agenda? What are the other topics?
- By when should I confirm my acceptance?

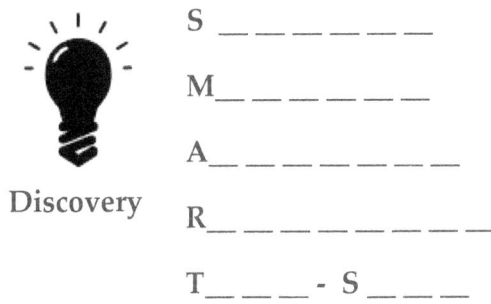

S __ __ __ __ __ __

M__ __ __ __ __ __

A__ __ __ __ __ __ __

Discovery R__ __ __ __ __ __ __ __

T__ __ __ - S __ __ __

Before we move on to some finer points of this exercise, let's look at five broad areas you can remember with the help of this *Smart Tool*.

Five broad areas for gathering the 'first facts':

- **Subject**
- **Mastery**
- **Audience**
- **Resources**
- **Time-slot**

Subject

The first and foremost step is to identify the subject of presentation. At this stage, it is not required to pin down the topic precisely, but to broadly capture the subject in a single sentence. If you were to tell someone about your ensuing talk, how would you put it? You can refine this later as you work through the stuff. We will work on this more in the next chapter as we arrive to the topic of your talk.

Mastery

Let's face it, the audience are more likely to pay attention to a speaker who they believe is credible. What brings credibility to the speaker is the mastery one has on the subject matter at hand. It need not essentially mean that you have a formal qualification, it could mean that you have conceptual soundness in the area or some story or experience to relate the subject. "Does the subject interest me? Does it relate to any voluntary work or specialised studies I have done? Do I have some interesting experience to share in this area?" Your answer to these questions signal your mastery. And your level of mastery gives you the initial confidence to take up the presentation. Though one would not like to take up subjects that are not their 'cup of tea', you will find veteran speakers delivering talks even on any subject they are asked to speak on. As you become a seasoned speaker, you would love talking to the extent that you will be able to bring in a new perspective to any topic you are asked to speak on by aptly connecting it with your personal story. But reserve unfamiliar subject matters for a later date.

To establish credibility, you don't have to build a lengthy 'intro' highlighting all you career milestones. But you need to give a thought about how to subtly bring it in the introductory part. As you build your presentation, try to link up an experience that shaped your talk or the legwork you have done relating to what you are going to tell them.

Audience

Though the first information about the audience can give you some basic facts, you may consider gathering more details for tweaking the contents to suit the audience: Why would they want to come and attend your presentation? What age group / demographic/ occupational profile do they belong to? What do the audience already know about the subject? What do they hope for from the time they spend listening? What are their concerns? What is likely to be their disposition to the subject matter?

Resources

It is about what is available at the venue vis-à-vis what you require to make your presentation effective. You should prepare a checklist of your requirements and check it with the resources available: What kind of seating is provided- theatre style or cluster seating? What kind of presentation aids you can use? Would you need a microphone? Are you going to use PowerPoint or will you be showing a video clipping. Do you need to access net connection while you present? In order to avoid last minute mishap, it is very important to check all these well in advance and adjust your presentation according to the available infra structure and presentation aids.

Timeslot and Timing

You need to be sure of the timeslot you have been allotted since the contents have to be fitted within the timeslot. If you are the only speaker, there could be some flexibility on this. But if you are to speak in a conference or seminar, where there are other speakers preceding and following you, you not only need to know and ensure that you stick to the timeslot. Getting to know the topics of other speakers will help in preparing your content without overlap and at the same time, build a linkage with other topics.

First Facts:

Check if you have gathered the basic particulars you need for starting your preparation

Checklist

Subject	☐ Do you have a clear idea of the subject? ☐ Can you describe your subject matter in a single sentence?
Mastery	☐ Are you passionate about this subject? ☐ Does the subject relate to your area of your experience or studies? ☐ Have you got a compelling story in this area? (consider your background/ experiences relating to the subject)
Audience	☐ Do you know about your audience - what is common to them- what background – why they are interested in this subject etc?
Resources	☐ Have you checked the availability of audio equipments, seating arrangements etc?
Time	☐ Date, time, venue ☐ Duration for your talk ☐ Agenda items and topics

4. Groundwork

You have got the 'first facts' and you are all set to start preparing your contents. Before you go and work through the details, there are a certain preliminary things that you need to mull over and have clarity in your head:

- Purpose or objective of your talk

- Topic

- Broad structure

Purpose – Your Intent Statement

Why do you want to deliver a talk? What do you intend to achieve? What would you like your audience to do by the end of your talk?

Though there could be more than one purpose, there is one that is predominant. Spell it out. Broadly, it could fall into one of the following:

1. **To inform or to update on progress:** Ceremonial presentations like introducing the speakers or event, delivering welcome address or vote of thanks etc., or even

presenting project reports and status updates are of simple type that essentially focus on providing information in an interesting way.

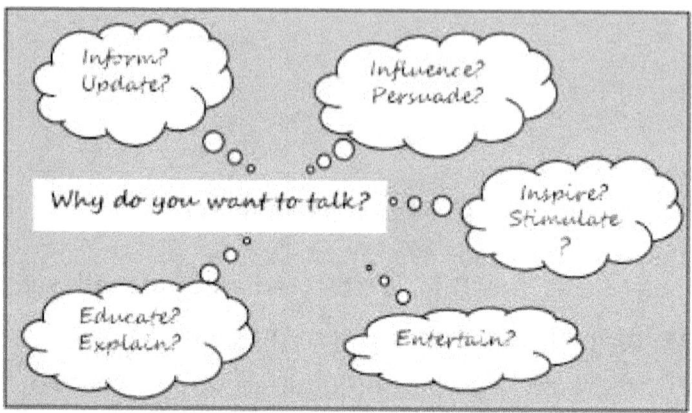

2. **To persuade or influence:** Your purpose would mainly be to persuade your audience, when you make presentations for product or brand promotion, sales pitch for offerings and services, product launches etc. You may need to influence the management when you present a new project or propose a policy change. When you want to raise capital for a business venture or seek support for your idea, you must be able to make winning presentations.

3. **To motivate or inspire:** Be it giving a pep talk to your team to enhance their drive for performance, or giving motivational speeches to large audience, your talk should be able to inspire the people and charge them with energy. behaviours

4. **To train, to educate or to explain:** Paper presentations in seminars and conferences, or lectures on different

disciplines are of a special type requiring expertise in the subject matter, whereas training would encompass all the above purposes since it is not only imparting knowledge to audience, but also inspiring them about the subject and persuading them to apply it in real life.

Intend Statement

Whatever you think is the main purpose, try to bring that in to the description of your subject. Writing an Intent Statement can set the direction for your preparation. Here are some examples of Intent Statements and try to identify the purpose category:

- To pitch in for a particular product by comparing its features and benefits with that of the competition

- To motivate a rural group to adopt better health and hygiene practices for a healthy living

- To train a group of managers to apply the smart tools for effective presentation

Now, think about a presentation you may like to give and then write your Intent Statement. Use this as a walk through to developing a real-life presentation.

Structure

Though the talk has to flow like one continuous stream, we can consider the structure of the talk as having three distinct parts:

- Opening: That is when you get their attention and ramp it up quickly as you get into to the mainframe. You can take roughly up to 10- 20% of your time, which means roughly around 4 to 5 minutes of a thirty minute presentation.

- Mainframe is what you deliver as the body of your talk. You need to spend a considerable part of 70 to 80% of your time on the mainframe.

- Closing: That is when sum up and conclude your talk. 10% or less of your talk time is ideal. A good speech is one that is shorter than the audience attention span.

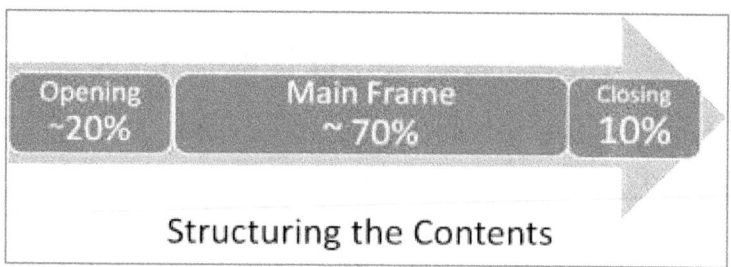

| Opening ~20% | Main Frame ~ 70% | Closing 10% |

Structuring the Contents

'What, Why & How' Framework:

Whatever be the subject matter, a presentation may need to essentially address the questions 'What?', 'Why?' and 'How?' of the subject matter. The purpose of your presentation will determine the extent of emphasis you will lay on each of the above questions.

- 'What?' is about the key message – it can be some knowledge or informational input. Think about those inputs that can benefit from the perspective of the audience. If the core purpose is 'to inform' then focus can be on addressing the 'Whats' of your subject.

- 'Why?' is the question that is predominant in the minds of audience: 'why is this important?' 'why should I pursue your line of thinking?' 'why should it be that way?' Addressing 'why' gives them the reason for listening to you and more particularly, to toe your line of thinking. If you want to be a persuasive speaker, you may need to consider the 'whys' from the perspective of the audience and provide a compelling argument.

- 'How?' Addressing the 'how' is more important if the purpose of the talk is to familiarise the participants with a new system or to train them on specific procedures.

Though you need to bear in mind these questions while preparing your contents, it would be too simplistic to think of providing the answers straight. You may need the use of right tools to gather your ideas and thoughts, prioritise and organise them in order and concoct them into a compelling story so as to achieve the purpose of your presentation. In the later chapters, we will discuss those tools that can help in developing your script.

But now, let's see how to grab the attention of the audience with a stimulating start.

5. 'Opening' Styles

'Well begun is half done.' The first few minutes are very crucial for your presentation to entice the audience into your topic. As you start, the people are still in their own inner world of distractions, judgments and opinions. In order to get their attention and arouse the interest in your topic, you need to quickly build a connect between their concerns and your purpose.

And when you have done this part well in building rapport with your listeners, your initial anxiety starts vanishing and your confidence level automatically goes up. Your focus now shifts to the topic and you start flowing with it unmindful of you. To make this happen, you need to be completely in charge with a thoroughly prepared 'opening'. You must have rehearsed it so well that it sounds like a comfortable conversation with your audience. Even many of the seasoned speakers do have their first few sentences well by-hearted, so that they focus their energy more on connecting with audience rather than on their spoken words.

Presentations are like T20 cricket games, where you have to pile up your 'runs' right from the first ball. Effective opening statements can quickly ramp up your score with the audience.

Plan an effective opening that provides the audience with an outline of the presentation you are about to give, informing them briefly of the points you will be making during your speech. Use anecdotes to break the ice and draw the audience into your speech in a familiar way.

Warm-ups

Here are some strategies for warming up the audience before jumping into the subject matter:

- complimenting the audience on a recent accomplishment of the group

- recalling the personal connect you have with the place, or institution, or occasion, or people

- greeting the audience in their native tongue (particularly if that is foreign to you)

- greeting appropriately on festival in the locality, if any, at that point in time

- talking about a moment in history (e.g: at this time, at this place, fifteen years ago...)

Kick-starts

Here are a few opening styles that can kick-start the topic and you can pick the one that works for you.

- **A Startling Statement/ Statistic:** A plain shocking fact well-related to the purpose of the talk can have a big influence on the audience.

  e.g.: "There is one death every four minutes due to road accident in the country and two wheelers account for 25% of them." How about an opener like this for a talk insisting upon on 'Helmet usage'.

- **Story/ personal anecdote:** Steve Jobs started his Commencement Address (2005) at Stanford University like this. *"Truth be told, I never graduated from college, and this is the closest I've ever gotten to a college graduation"*

- **Straight into WIIFM Factor:** If you are going to present something that has concrete take-aways, then you can think of a simple one liner that can capture the WIIFM (what-is-in-it-for-me) factor.

  e.g.: "Today you will learn three most closely guarded secrets of the most wealthiest person in the world".

- **Question:** Consider asking yourself a question that could be in the minds of audience and go on answering your own question. This is found to be an effective way to draw their thinking into your topic. Be sure to consider your audience and the things they would wonder about, and phrase your questions so you answer those things for them, while at the same time advancing your message and your goals for the presentation.

E.g.: *"You might wonder why such a dry topic interests me…"*; or *"When I started to look at this issue, I asked myself …"*

- **Time Travel:** Taking them forward in time and constructing a scenario connected with your topic can be a good stimulator. Similarly, you can travel back in time to recall the state of affairs then to indicate the kind of progress or regress in a particular area

e.g.: *"10 years from now, you won't be carrying a wallet with you when you travel"*

Say 'No' to worn-out and apologetic openers

These are some quick ways to lose your audience and you need to be wary of them and avoid them at all costs.

'I am not a good speaker, but anyway….'

"Today I have been asked to speak on…'

'You might have already heard the story I am going to tell you, yet I would,….'

'I don't want to stand between you and the interesting events lined up for the evening'

Framework for openers

The next two chapters will provide you with a framework for organising your opening part of the presentation.

6. A Rousing Start

A stirring or startling start can be one where the first few sentences slightly shake off the comfort of audience members by painting a shocking scenario or presenting the disturbing state of affairs. Once they are sensitized to the gravity of the situation, give them a big picture comparison. Then go on to assuage their concern and assure them how you are going to help them through your presentation.

Let us start with an example of a 'startling opening'. You can find out the *Smart Tool* for yourself by guessing the words at the beginning of each paragraph. This tool is discussed in later part of the chapter

Demo

"Good Morning everybody!

S _ _ _ _ U _

Before we go, let's take stock. How good are you in getting your message across? Can you convince an unknown group of people to your view point or sell a product to them through a presentation? How would you rate yourself on this ability, say on a scale of 1 to 10? Be honest and tell me where you are. Who would say 'I am a perfect 10' or anyone anywhere close?

M__ __ __   **P** __ __ __ __ __ __

You are not an odd one out. Most people out there in the professional world, have this problem when it comes to presentation. Everyone - every professional, every manager, why even every student - do very well know how vital it is for their professional success. The higher you climb up the professional ladder, the more essential it becomes. Also the more you avoid presentation, the more scary it becomes. Though everyone wants to be better at it, everyone prefers to stay with the problem.

A__ __ __ __ __

It is not where you stand that matters, but it is where you want to go from here. Where would you like to move this rating, say in the next one month, so that you can make an impact on every audience you speak to and emerge more and more competent and confident with every presentation you make. You want to make it a Perfect10, don't you?

And I am here to help you with that. It is just a matter of knowing some simple tools and applying them with rigour. Once you test your skill on the stage and get the taste of it, you'll begin loving the stage and start looking for opportunities to be on stage.

R__ __ - **U**__

I am going to share with you those tools – there are not many, but just nine of them- that will do the magic to your presentations. These are simple tools that help you right from the word 'go'- that is the moment you give your nod for a speaking assignment till the point of completing your presentation. These *Smart Tools* will help you in gathering the required information, structuring your thoughts and ideas and will help you in preparing your stuff and delivering it with impact.

T__ __ __ __ __

My promise may look lofty to you. These tools are well-tested and proven. But how can you make them work? They will work for you only when you work on them. Apply them; put them to test when you deliver your next talk and see the results for yourself. That will get you the value out of the time you are going to spend here. All I need is your undivided attention for the next thirty minutes. If you have questions to ask or doubts to get clarified, ensure to take them with me during the 'question time' towards the close of my talk.

Now take your guess:

S __ __ __   U __

M__ __ __   P __ __ __ __ __ __

A__ __ __ __ __

Discovery   R__ __ - U__

T__ __ __ __ __

Five steps to a Startling Opening

Tool

- **Stir up**
- **Mega picture**
- **Assure**
- **Refer Links**
- **Treaty**

- **Stir up:** Start with something that can stir up the audience emotionally and can surface their unconscious concern.

- **Mega picture:** Paint the mega picture of the state of affairs – set the context- how the situation is presenting itself and what audience need to be concerned about.

- **Assure:** Assure them what will happen at the end of your talk that will remove their concerns and apprehensions. Share your objectives and purpose of the talk in such a way that they come as assurance and promises of achieving

- **Run-up:** Give a run-up of how the 'talk' is going to go. You can give them a quick snapshot of your talk - let them know what you are going to cover and what is the scope of the topic

- **Treaty:** Create a contract or Treaty with the audience on the specific expectations from them during and after your talk for realising your promises.

A Startling Start:

Do you think you can consider 'opening' with a provocative start for your topic and the kind of audience?

Checklist

Stir up	☐ Have you got a question, story or a quote that is positively provoking? ☐ Does your opening trigger the need in the participants for the new knowledge/ information you are going to provide through the presentation?
Mega-picture	☐ Have you provided the mega-picture (prevailing larger scenario) relating to the concern you have raised among the audience? ☐ Do you give them the feel 'you are not alone'?
Assure	☐ What is your promise and purpose that can help them overcome their concern? ☐ What they can expect to achieve by the end of your talk?
Run-up	☐ Have you given a Run-up of your talk? ☐ Have you given the scope of the topic?
Treaty	☐ Have you spelt out the terms of Treaty (you expect from them)? : ☐ Participation: when to ask questions? Attention, participation, keeping off distractions (switching off mobile phone and such other requests) ☐ Actions required: what you expect of them post the presentation? ☐ Time duration: how long is your talk?

7. Or A Proven Start

Let us look at another way to start – a more conventional way, that has been proven to work. Dissect the 'opening' of any well-structured talk and you are sure to find at least two or three elements of this framework.

The following example uses a *Smart Tool* that can be used for yourself for crafting your 'opening'. Guess the tool and think of ways of applying to your own presentation.

Demo

S _ _ _ _   I _ _ _ _ _ _ _

A man goes to the physician and shares his concern: "*Doctor, I think my wife is developing deafness off late. These days she is not responding to me. I don't know how to tell her because I am not sure. How do I check whether she has become deaf?*" The doctor gives him an idea: "*When she is not looking at you, ask her some question from about thirty feet. If she is not responding, then repeat it from about 20 feet, then from 10 feet. If still she is not replying to you, then you can take it as confirmed."* When the man goes home that evening, he sees her busy in kitchen. He thinks it is the right time. He asks her in a slightly loud voice, *'darling, what is it for dinner?'* Getting no response, he repeats it twice, as doctor had suggested, from different distances. Dead silence. He gets close to her, gently puts his arm around her shoulder and tells her, *'hi dear, I asked you what you are making for dinner, but...'* Before he could complete, she turns around and yells at him, *'how many times should I tell you - it is only the usual roti-sabji'.*

M__ __ __ __ __ __

This is the problem with most of us in leadership roles in the organisations. We somehow, assume the problem is with the other person when things do not happen our way. When people don't respond to our communication, we not only assume the problem is with them, but we go about solving it by sending them for training or counseling them, and if nothing works, even firing them. But hardly do we ask ourselves: does the problem lie with me? In any communication, the onus lies with the sender and if you want to get the intended results, then you need to take charge – charge of not only what you say and how you say it, but get to understand how it landed out there.

A__ __

That is why we are here today- we are here to understand the barriers that come from our communication styles and how we can become conscious of such flaws. Not only that, we will also see what are the ways available for you to get rid of these breakdowns and become more effective in getting your message across the way you meant. That is the purpose of my talk.

R__ __ __ __ __

Let us deal with the barriers of communication one by one. I will be sharing examples for each type of communication breakdown through a short video clip which will be followed by a quick check with you in identifying what caused the breakdown. Then we will look at the ways of overcoming them.

T__ __ __ __

The theme for my talk this evening is *'Seven Communication Breakdowns'* and we will be dwelling on this for the next 30 minutes.

Now take your guess:

Discovery

S __ __ __ __   I __ __ __ __ __ __ __ __

M__ __ __ __ __

A__ __

R__ __ __ __ __

T__ __ __ __

Five Step Opening

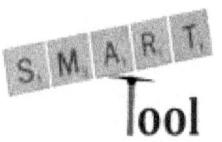
Tool

- Spark interest
- Motive
- Aim
- Range
- Topic /Time

Here is the SMART Tool for making the 'opening' of your talk:

- **Spark interest:** Think up something that can stimulate the interest of the audience and can deeply connect with the topic - an exciting experience, inspiring quote, intriguing information or a real life incident.

- **Motive:** What is the audience's **Motive** for attending the talk? – the big concern or reason that they all share? Connect your start with their need and then build on.

- **Aim:** Share the purpose or **Aim** – how their need will be addressed. State the objectives as to where they will be at the end of your talk.

- **Range:** What can they expect to listen? What areas are you going to cover? Give a **Range** of things that will be covered in your talk. Set the scope of your talk

- **Topic:** Clarify the **Topic** and **Time** length of your talk

A Conventional Start:

Consider how you can structure your 'opening' into this framework.

Checklist

Spark Interest	☐ Quick welcome and a brief self- intro (if not already done by the organisers) ☐ Does your 'Opening statement' immediately spur the interest? ☐ Does it establish a quick rapport with the audience?
Motive	☐ Does it connect with the need/ concern of the audience? ☐ Do you have a question to affirm that their concern/ need is in sync with your conjecture?
Aim	☐ Is the Purpose spelt out in terms of 'at the end of the talk, you will be able to….'? ☐ Have you clarified your expectations from the audience (when to ask questions etc)?
Range	☐ Have you covered the Scope of your talk – what will be coming up? ☐ And what will not be covered– any specific item relating to the topic? (e.g. sans PPT in the title of the book)
Topic	☐ Have you reiterated the topic for effect? ☐ Also do they know how much of their time you need?

8. Design Your Main Frame

Our Joe, who has been invited by his alma mater to deliver a talk, called up the college again and systematically gathered all the essential 'first facts' and set out to start his preparation.

He spent a few minutes thinking about what the ideal topic could be and he felt he had a number of ideas coming to his mind. He thought he would put them into his draft speech and opened a new 'Word' file in his laptop. As he keyed in the opening words, 'good evening, ladies and gentlemen!', there were more and different ways of addressing the gathering: 'emerging leaders!' 'friends of my alma mater!' etc. As the dilemma of whether he should use formal salutations and protocols or use a generic one, he thought he would first prepare the broad contents and so he switched to PowerPoint. At the same time, he also thought he should google a bit to explore the topic and soon he was lost in a quagmire.

Do you think that is right way to go about preparing the contents? What would you suggest Joe?

Obviously, writing down a speech or preparing slides on PowerPoint cannot be the first step for preparation. Because, if you start writing, you tend to get bogged down with finer details like addressing protocols, styling of the talk, grammatical correctness or factuality of data and so on. Since you are already familiar with the subject- hopefully so, since you have accepted to talk on it- you should start with capturing what you already know and then prioritise and organise those ideas. Then you can convert them into script or prompt cards and necessary visuals as may be needed.

Structuring the Contents

Let's look at a systematic approach to preparing the contents and also some of the tools available for structuring and organising the material data.

The following five steps will help you structure your contents for the main portion of your talk:

1. Gather the **Stuff**: The raw materials for your talk are the ideas, thoughts and knowledge that lie in your head in a random and scattered manner. The first step is to collect and gather the stuff in your head and capture them on to a paper.

2. **Cull the Main points:** When you have reasonably gathered all the points that you have on the subject and also points that you have collected to fill any gaps, you

need to cull out the vital points that can contribute to the purpose of your presentation by screening and weeding out the superfluous stuff and arriving at *main points* to focus in the talk

3. **Arrange them:** Once you have the main points and the key sub-points, you have to *arrange* them in an order so that it flows in a coherent and logical manner.

4. **Enliven your talk:** Now that you have got a basic skeletal stuff, you have to breathe life into it by using the right kind of rhetorical and persuasive methods to get the buy in from your audience.

5. **Build Transition signposts:** : When you give a finishing touch to your script, you need to create verbal signposts to help audience navigate through your talk.

Tools and Steps for Structuring Contents

- **Spray diagram**
- **MoSCoW**
- **Arrange in order**
- **Reason & Resonance**
- **Transitions**

Now let's see some of the tools and methods you can use to carry out these five steps.

Spray Diagram

When you try to put your ideas in full and complete sentences, your focus is on writing and you tend to lose the train of ideas that arise from previous ideas. Spray diagram is one simple and easy-to-use method to capture the thoughts and ideas as they come in without losing them.

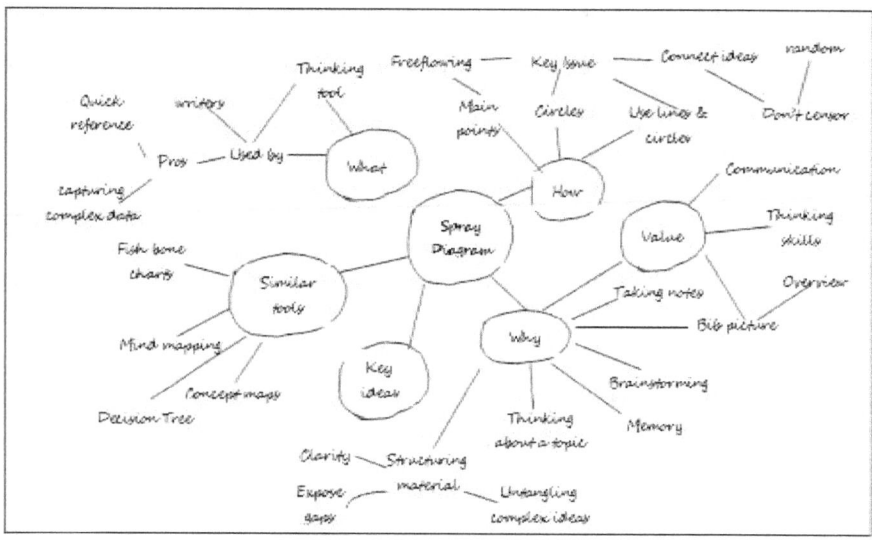

Creating Spray Diagram:

1. Do this exercise during your best time of the day i.e. when you are at your creative best as per your bio-rhythm and do it quickly and fluently without interruptions.

2. Take a big sheet of paper (A3 size paper or a flip-chart) and use it in landscape format.

48

3. Write the subject in the centre and encircle it.

4. Think about your subject not just from your own angle, but from the likely view points of your likely audience.

5. As ideas come into your mind, branch out from centre and jot down your ideas. Don't censor the ideas now.

6. Use key words only to represent each idea.

7. If any point or idea is connected to another, connect them with lines or as branching out from the main idea.

As you keep going, you will be surprising yourself with newer ideas and thoughts and keep at it until you feel you have exhausted enough. Hang the chart on the wall or in some place visible to you and keep adding the thoughts as they come. Allow the chart to remain there for a day or two and as it incubates in your mind and as you come up with newer ideas, keep coming back to the chart and adding them on. You will now have sufficient raw material to work on.

Main points: Cull them from the Clutter

When you complete the spray diagram, you will have far more information than you can carry in your presentation. If you try to cram too many points in to your talk, it becomes too superficial and falls flat. Instead of going wider and covering too many points, take a few points and dwell deeper; give more details; support with more examples. So make sure that you have arrived at three to five main points before you go to the next stage.

In order to prioritise these main points, you may use the Pareto Principle, according to which 20% of your stuff will have 80% impact. So cull out that Vital 20% and discard the remaining trivial 80%. To apply the Pareto principle to your spray diagram, you use the tool known as **MoSCoW** which is a mnemonic for **M**ust, **S**hould, **C**ould and **W**ould. This method can be used for distilling the **Main points** from your spray diagram and weeding out all the excess.

Your 'spray diagram' has all that you **would** like to say or more

If you want to say all you know, you will sound hollow.

Think of what you **could** say to help them.

Say only what **should** go in. Address

WIIFM of your audience.

Focus on purpose.

Cut all surplus.

Retain only

What are

Musts

As you edit the spray diagram, mark C for the 'could ideas' and cut off the rest and as you go on you will have only those points marked M (Musts) and the

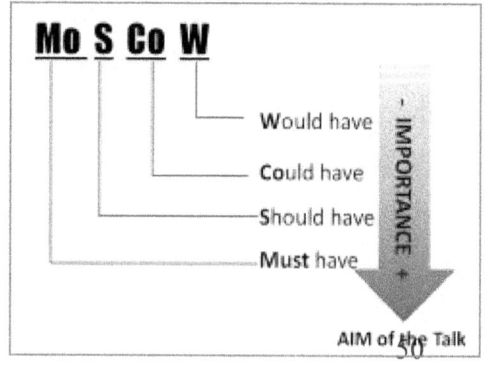

rest are cut off. If you have more than three to five Main points at this stage, you need to again filter it to bring it a maximum of 5. You need to be ruthless.

Arrange

Arranging the prioritised points in a logical and coherent flow is the next step. Here are some guidelines to bear in mind when organising your main points and sub-points

o   Order of familiarity: Taking the story from what is known to the unknown and new will be easy to follow

o   Order of complexity: It always helps to start with the simple and basic concepts that are building blocks of a complex issue you are going to take them to.

o   Observation to theory: If you are going to talk of an abstract theory, can you relate it to something that can be observed or experienced in real life?

As you start putting them in order, take a note of the associated ideas, stories and examples that come up in your mind. Also note those points you may need to do more research or gather more details so as to convincingly build your storyline.

Reason & Resonance

Having got your major points for your talk, all you have is just the bare skeleton. You now, have to add flesh and breathe life into it.   A good talk appeals to both our head and heart and has a right blend of emotional touch and logical appeal.

Some talks are meant to be persuasive while some may intend to inspire and motivate people. When you are more keen on persuading people to buy your point of view or a product you sell, you will focus more on placing the facts before them and provide evidence to support your point.

If your intention is to motivate them to adopt a new attitude or behaviour, you may need to instigate them, instil confidence in them and be charged up about what you are saying. Your talk has to resonate emotionally with your audience.

Whatever be the case, if you want to create emotional resonance in your talk and also provide solid reasons to back your side of argument, you have got a range of tools to pick from in the succeeding two chapters (Chapter 9 and 10)

Transitions

The speech cannot be delivered as one large lump. It has to be in small digestible chunks that flow seamlessly one after another. To flow it seamlessly, you need to plan transition from the 'opening' to the 'main frame' or from 'main frame' to 'closing' and also the transitions from one key point to another within them.

Signposts: Signposts are to a speech what chapter headings are to a book. To help audience sail along with you, these transitions from one point to another can be indicated by verbal or non-verbal signposts. The signposts help the audience understand the progression of the talk and also take the inputs in smaller chunks. Importantly, transitions draw the audience's attention to the process of the presentation as well as its content.

Here are some examples of using verbal signposts:

- *"Let's now move on to …"*
- *"The next point I would like to …"*
- *"In sequel to what we saw earlier concerning …"*
- *"As we are coming to the concluding part,…"*

If you have not built in verbal signposts, when there is a transition from a point to the next, you may use non-verbal indicators, like giving a longer pause, moving to a different area before opening the next topic, or turning over to the next flip chart or changing a slide.

Design Your Talk:

Check how you can use this approach to develop the contents of your talk

Checklist

Spray diagram	☐ Have you captured all your thoughts, ideas and points you have relating to the subject? ☐ Did you explore more sources like internet, books to pick relevant points? ☐ Have you given enough incubation time to get your insights and dormant ideas on the subject?
Main points	☐ Have you done a Pareto to cull out the vital 20% which have a great relevance to your purpose? ☐ Have you screened your points to pick five to seven major points for the presentation?
Arrange	☐ Have you arranged your key points in a logical and coherent flow?
Resonance	☐ Have you used appropriate methods to breathe 'life into the script'?
Transitions	☐ Have you built in verbal signposts to indicate transitions from one point to another? ☐ Have you got clear indications to signal transition from 'opening' to 'mainframe' and from 'mainframe' to 'closing'?

9. "Prove It To Me!"

When you are presenting to persuade your audience and trying your best to move them to action, it is important that you provide enough factual details and evidence to support your point by the way of statistical data, research findings and relevant examples. Though too much detail can make your talk dreary, you need to consider how to handle these tools in a lively manner. When you dwell on the details using any of the following methods, ensure that it goes well with the overall story.

Tools for persuasive approach

- Statistics
- Merits & Demerits
- Actual use (demo)
- Reference
- Testimonials

Statistics

Statistics can be effective for convincing the people. At the same time, too much of it can make the presentation lifeless and impersonal. When you put the numbers in a new perspective, you can make even the complex data understandable and memorable.

For instance, if you say *hedge funds manager and super trader John Paulson earned $ 4.9 billion in 2009*, it doesn't capture the imagination. But the effect could be totally different, when you say the same thing like this: *'if you are earning Rs. sixty lakh per annum, which is a decent income, all that John Paulson would need to earn the same is around 10.5 seconds. Come to think of it, at this rate you may need 69,000 years to earn his level of income.'*

When you use visuals to show the statistical charts and graphs, you can make them interesting by using info-graphics. Info-graphics are a special kind of visual representation where you use you use relevant pictures in proportionate sizes in graphs instead of showing just plain bars in histograms. For example, if you are talking about the growth oil production during a period of five years, you can use the picture of a barrel with different sizes proportionate to the quantum.

Visit the websites, that use interactive info-graphics and you can get brilliant ideas for breathing life into your numbers and personalising them.

Merits (& demerits too?)

It is a misconception that we should only talk about the merits and positives of our case and we should not even acknowledge the negative points. We often nurture a fear that the audience may hold on to the negatives and reject our later argument. But if your conviction is weak, then you will not be able to offer a convincing refutation to the negatives you acknowledge.

If you are able to provide a strong refutation to the apparent drawbacks that are expected to be in minds of your audience, then you would have answered those likely questions that would arise towards the end of your talk and may leave a bitter note

Actual use (Demo)

Nothing like showing it live- what Steve Jobs has always been at his best. His product launch presentations are something to learn from for anyone who wants to introduce a product in a lively manner. When you show your audience the actual usage or a product 'demo', it is imperative that you start with 'why' before you go to 'how'- why this product or offering is required – what problems it can solve, and how it stands out from the rest. Then go about your demo - show the actual use at its best without dragging into drab technical details. Then go on and show something really cool before closing with a few unique benefits very succinctly.

Reference

You can enhance the persuasive effect of your talk, if you can support your points with references from business or trade journals or periodicals, research reports, books or acknowledged experts. Citing reliable sources of information to back your view helps in reinforcing your point. Or, if you have first-hand knowledge by conducting a survey or research, share your findings authentically.

Testimonials

Testimonial lends a good deal of credibility since it comes out of the first-hand experience of the person giving the testimonial. But the question is: How do you embed a testimonial into your presentation? A simple way of course, is to neatly print the testimonials along with the name and identity of the customer and provide it as a handout. During the Presentation you can refer to any catchy point mentioned by them and have the handout distributed. You need to make sure that the testimonial you use strengthens your pitch and goes well with your target audience. It is important that you get the customer's permission beforehand for using their comments.

If you can afford to produce short and appropriate video of testimonials, then you can use it as a part of your presentation to reinforce your point.

Tools for Persuasion:

Consider which of the following tools would apply to your presentation. How can you effectively use in your presentation to persuade your listeners?

Checklist

Statistics	☐ Do you have statistical data to support your case?
Merits	☐ Can you talk about demerits of your case and then elucidate on how the merits not only invalidate the demerits but supersede them far more?
Actual show (demo)	☐ Do you have something live to show? Can you demo your offering?
Reference	☐ What trusted sources of knowledge, can you cite as reference to back your view?
Testimonials	☐ Can you have a client or a customer share a positive experience of your offering?

10. "Inspire Me!"

When you build a rock-solid case supported by facts and numbers, you may think that you have got enough to prove your point and convince your audience. But when it comes to human decisions, there is always subtle, yet strong, play of emotions and perceptions. So it is vital to consider also those aspects that appeal to the heart. Resonating with your audience emotionally calls for touching the right chords. Great orators are adept at using those tools, what are known as rhetoric devices. Greeks are known to have developed many rhetoric ways which are effective even today.

Tools for Emotional Appeal

- **Story**
- **Metaphor**
- **Antithesis**
- **Rhetorical questions**
- **Triads**

Story

There is so much emphasis on 'story telling' that some organisations have started considering it as one of the vital leadership competencies. Stories do help in grabbing the attention of audience and make the presentation more lively. Stories do help in evoking the right emotions of audience and in communicating complex ideas. When you weave the story with the language and imagery that paints a picture in front of them, you can be sure of winning their hearts. In the next chapter, we will look at a tool that can help you develop your story.

Metaphor

A metaphor is a creative way of depicting a thing as something else. It is a way of connecting something new with something that is familiar. When Kodak first introduced camera into the market, it used the metaphor 'mirror with a memory' which made it easy for the people to comprehend what the new contraption called camera would do. Metaphors can thus, help introducing a new or unfamiliar idea, concept or product.

Altering the Organising Metaphors: The world-views we hold in our mind that determine our actions are revealed by the language we use to represent it, which are known as *organising metaphors*. For example, sales people, who view the market as 'price war', find it tough to sell their premium product because they hold the view that their product is priced higher than the competition and believe that competitive pricing can only boost the sale. This organising metaphor can be altered with a more positive approach like 'values sell' or 'people bring in the difference' provided you are able to provide compelling evidence and success stories.

Replacing the organising metaphors of people may not be easy, since people tend to cling on to their world views. Yet, you can persuade them to consider a different viewpoint by pointing out the flaws in the existing metaphors with evidence and providing them with a more reliable one .

'Nation's development is a government job and people hardly have anything to do with it' is one of the most commonly-held organising metaphor by the general public. *'One step by every Indian is one and a quarter billion steps for our country'*, can be a powerful attempt to change the organising metaphor of the public, **provided** it is spoken by a person at a level of authority holding charge of the nation and, if uttered with right emotional sincerity, and at the right occasion to get the attention of the entire country.

This is what Prime Minister Narendra Modi spoke, when he addressed the nation on the 68th Independence Day on Aug 15, 2014 from the ramparts of the Red Fort, *'Brothers and Sisters, Don't you think the citizens of the country need to take part in the building of the nation? Imagine, if each of you, my countrymen, move one step forward, then our country moves by one and a quarter billion steps forward'*.

Antithesis

'And so, my fellow Americans, ask not what the country can do for you; ask what you can do for the country', the words spoken by US President JFK in 1961 are remembered even today. This is an elegant use of antithesis.

As you can see, antithesis is nothing but placing two opposing thoughts together in the same sentence or same construction. Though it is rarely used today, because of its dramatic element, if you are creative enough you can add colour to your presentation with antithesis.

Rhetorical questions

"If you prick us, do we not bleed? if you tickle us, do we not laugh? if you poison us, do we not die? and if you wrong us, shall we not revenge?" Look at the way Shakespeare has crafted the opening of Shylock's speech with a series of rhetoric questions in the *Merchant of Venice*. Shylock starts with these questions to justify his revenge against Antonio.

Rhetoric questions are those questions the speaker poses for the sole purpose of producing effect. The intention of asking such questions is not for getting a resounding yes from your listeners, but rather a silent agreement to your standpoint and to draw them into your argument.

Business presentations are replete with opportunities for the use of rhetoric questions: *'Do you want to sell a commodity that is at the mercy of the competition all the time to get its price? Or, do you want to sell a product that commands a premium in the market and gives you the pride of being a market leader? And today, we are here to discuss and implement the strategies to rise our product as incontestable market leader'*

Triads

Julius Ceaser's *'veni, vidi, vici'* (I came, I saw, I conquered) is a well-worn example for a triad. A triad or tricolon (also termed as Rule of Threes) is just a grouping of three items. Greek orators are found to have been fond of using triads. Triads still remain an effective way to get a grip on the attention of audience.

Triad seems to be a favourite of US President Barrack Obama and we can spot as many as twenty two triads in his Inauguration speech alone. The two minute Gettysburg address of Abraham Lincoln in 1863 is one of the most celebrated speeches in history and the speech is interspersed with a beautiful triad that has come to stay *'... this nation shall have a new birth of freedom, and that government of the people, by the people, for the people shall not perish from the earth.*

You could have noticed the deft usage of triad by Indian Prime Minister Narendra Modi. *'Democracy, Demography and Demand'* is a famous triad he used during his rousing rock-star speech at Madison Square to the Indian Diaspora to indicate the three factors that make India attractive for investors.

Triads can be effectively used in business context too. A marketing head of a FMCG company used a triad, *'Pride, Perseverance, Premium'* during his key note address in a sales conference which later became the motto for the company.

11. Weave Your Story

The following example uses a *Smart Tool* that can be used for yourself for crafting your 'story'. Guess the tool and think of ways to applying it to your own story.

Demo

Let's start straight away with a sample- a simple old story retold. Narrator is a new-gen Crow- yes, **the Thirsty Crow**. I ask you to bear with the extra exaggeration used in the story to bring out the effect.

S _ _ _ _ _ _

My throat was going dry. I had not had a sip of water for days. My village is in complete drought. I had drifted away from my community in search of water. My feathers were totally sapped and could not hold my body in the air anymore.

M_ _ _ _ _ _ _

But I didn't give up. I went on crawling on the ground in the scorching sun. I saw a pond of water a few feet away and crawled near it only to find it was just a mirage. Again to my luck, I saw a mud pot at a distance. I immediately recalled the story my grandma had told me long back –how she drank the pittance of water at the bottom of the pot by her brilliant idea which even humans had recognised and taught their children. So I dragged my feet to the pot and peeped inside. Lo, the pot was bone dry. I was soon losing hope. As I was about to give up, I found a mangled plastic bottle half-filled with water. I thought I would use my grandma's idea and started picking the stones lying around. Alas, the stones were still too big to be dropped into the bottle. At last, I saw a human creature; it was drinking coconut water through a long stick-like thing. Humans are our big hope since they help us with their penchant for littering.

"A_ _" M _ _ _ _ _

After emptying the coconut, it threw away stick-like thing. Why not try that thing? I just picked that stick-like contraption, shoved into the bottle and tried to suck the water. What a luck? Water started flowing into my mouth. *Aha, I can do it.* I should tell my grandma, when I get home.

R_ _ _ _ _ _ _

Now I was full of energy and started flying around. I felt light again and enjoyed floating in the air. I would never again lose my birdliness for want of few drops of water. In my newfound energy, I flew across the mountain which was a forbidden act in my crow-community. What a surprise? I saw a huge stream of water flowing incessantly – just only a few miles away from the spot where I was languishing for water only a few minutes ago.

T__ __ __ __ __ __

Come on, my crows, you need not be thirsty any more. I can lead you all to a whole new world of water, where you will never be thirsty any more. All you need to do is to take that one vital step - to step out of your comfort zone and fly with me beyond the mountain.

When you do it with your story, you can exaggerate on the intensity of the problem or struggle, but you need to be rather subtle when you talk of your achievement and if possible, bring in an element of self-deprecating humour, which can indicate a sense of humility.

A similar structure can be thought of, when you want to talk of how your startup came about or how you launched a new product – the tough challenges you faced –the trials and tribulations you went through- how you triumphed over them – and what promises it holds for the future.

Now take your guess:

Discovery

S __ __ __ __ __ __

M__ __ __ __ __ __ __

"A__ __" M __ __ __ __ __

R__ __ __ __ __ __ __

T__ __ __ __ __ __ __

You must have got it. Here's the Smart Tool to build your persuasive story:

Five Steps for Crafting Your Story

- **Struggle**
- **Meander**
- **'Aha' moment**
- **Revival**
- **Tomorrow**

Struggle

Build a narrative around a 'struggle' the protagonist in your story (you, your team, your organisation or the person you are talking about) was going through that relates to the purpose of the talk. Make it personal.

Meander

Dwell on how the hero, let's say 'you', meandered towards finding a solution- the various options you tried, the strategies you thought up, the actions you took and how all these efforts went in vain. Build up to create a keenness to know how you solved your problem at last.

'Aha' Moment

Break that 'aha' moment –that wonderful idea, or that turning point that ended all you woes. Share it with full exuberance-

share how you felt at that moment and how things started looking for you.

Revival

Focus on the recovery, the renewal and the resurgence. Talk about how the whole picture started looking bright. There is no looking back then on. Talk about the developments from then on and how positive the world started looking.

Tomorrow

So, what does the future have in store? How the people listening to you are going to benefit by your experience. What is the new possibility?

Build Your Story:

Do you have a compelling story that can fit into this framework?

Checklist

Struggle	☐ What is the big struggle? ☐ Where were you stuck? ☐ What was holding you back? ☐ Where it all started? ☐ How were you feeling?
Meanders	☐ How did you go about? Confused? Trying different ways? ☐ What options you had? ☐ Wanted to withdraw?
"Aha" moment	☐ What was the breakthrough? ☐ How did it come about?
Revival	☐ What changed for you? ☐ What changed around you? ☐ How did the people look at you?
Tomorrow	☐ How does the future look like now? ☐ What are the promises for tomorrow? ☐ How does your story address the 'wiifm' (what's in it for me?) factor of the audience?

12. Get Back to Centre Stage

Should you use PPT or not?

Today PowerPoint(PPT) is ubiquitous. Coming from the time, when preparing the transparencies used to be the most arduous task and using the OHP (overhead projector) used to be a key skill for the presenters, I do fully get what the PPT has done to our Presenter' world – the power it has put in our hands, the ease and comfort it has vested us with. But the extent of ease is so much that, when one is required to give a presentation, the first thing one does is to pull out a ready one from the internet and customize it. One cannot deny that PPT has taken the centre-stage and the presenter has been relegated to the side, if not the back

When you take shelter under the over-powering effect of PPT, you don't have the opportunity to feel the power of the spoken word that gives you the thrill of a speaker. Though I have been a great fan of PPT and use a great deal of it during my training sessions, I feel best way to hone one's Presentations Skills during the learning stage is to try and do it without PPT. If you want to use PPT, do use it to reinforce ideas on the listeners rather than as a crutch.

But Visuals do play a vital part in creating impact and you certainly have to find innovative ways of using them in your presentations. Let us look at some of the other kinds of visuals and support materials that can add effect to your talk session:

Flip chart

I have always found a sheaf of newsprint paper clipped on to an easel stand useful in my training sessions. It helps in recording the thoughts and key points as I go along and also to quickly acknowledge any good point that comes from the audience. Flipcharts can be used only when you have a small audience of, say, around 25 people or less. But remember if you want to record as you go about your presentation, you need to have a good legible handwriting and you should be able to write in bold block big letters so that it is easy to read even by the last benchers. Otherwise, you can also use pre-prepared sheets with key points and you can use it alongside your presentation for showing the progression from one main point to the next by turning the sheet.

Clinton Swaine is a globally well-known name in experiential games. It was an enriching experience for me to be in his 3-day 'Play To Win' training. Throughout the entire training, he used only flip-charts and absolutely no PowerPoint. He has an inimitable style of using flipcharts. If you want to use flipcharts like Swaine, some questions you need to ask yourself: Can I write without turning my back to the audience? Can I continue my talk as I write? Do I have a legible handwriting and can I write in big, block letters? Can I capture my thoughts on flipchart in crisp and precise words, without a single superfluous word?

You can also 'ghost' things onto the chart, by pre-writing it faintly with pencil which is not visible to the audience and you can go over it with marker during the presentation. It will be impressive to see the free-hand sketches emerging out of your pen as you make your presentation.

White Board

Most of what holds good for flipcharts also apply to white boards as well. Goes unsaid that you need to have a good and legible handwriting. If you are good at free-hand sketching, you can creatively depict your message in some simple line sketches. Be it flipchart or keyboard, bear in mind that you don't block their view or turn your back while writing and also to convey it in as few words as possible.

Electronic whiteboards: These days electronic whiteboards are being used widely. While you can use them to project your presentation, you can also write on them and can save your writings to serve as handouts. These whiteboards are touch sensitive, you can move text around on them. If you are required to use e-whiteboards, then it is important you have had enough practice beforehand.

Video Clips

Short and well-shot and relevant video clips can prove to have a very stimulating effect. Tell the audience beforehand what the video is about and what specifically to look for so that they don't miss the point.

Props

Props are any physical object you use in your presentation for effect. They can be quite simple things, or really gimmicky and surprising. Or, they may be special objects that you may need to bring for a demo. Your creativity and imagination will determine what you do with a prop. Simple prop might include a newsletter you printed with handmade paper or a small gadget you developed, that has relevance to the topic. If you are creative enough, you may even device ways of using the common objects that are available in the hall. I have seen a speaker borrowing a series of spectacles from the audience and wearing them one over the other until his view became totally blurred to see what was in front of him. Through this, he was metaphorically demonstrating that our view of reality is blurred by the filters of our experience.

Posters

Adorning the walls and the backdrop of the stage with well-designed posters appropriate to the topic can set the mood of your audience.

13. Rehearse it like Real

'If you are prepared, 95% of the fear of speaking will leave you; you need the other 5% to keep you humble'

- Don Aslett

'Do not memorize your speech', is what is suggested by many authorities on public speaking including Dale Carnegie, the doyen of public speaking.

'Many of our best and most popular TED talks have been memorized word for word', says Chris Anderson, Curator at Ted.

You may wonder why this contradiction. On the contrary, there is no contradiction at all. If you just memorize the script and try to deliver it on the stage, you will do a shoddy job, because there will not be life in it. It would be like the way the school children recite the mugged up poems. And since your memory may not be good as children, there is all possibility that you forget the next line, and fumble there in front of the audience. No speaker would ever want an embarrassment of that kind.

Mere memorizing and parroting it back is definitely not going to help, but if you are prepared to put in the same kind of efforts like what a TED speaker does, then you can go ahead and memorize.

Let us understand that there are three ways of using the memory:

1. **Repeat:** Memorize and repeat it back. Only memory and no emotion or creativity is involved in this.

2. **Reproduce:** Memorize, try it and adjust the tone of voice, tempo and modulations, recite it from your heart. You establish an emotional connect with the script. Even when the same music is played by an orchestra many times, we still find them appealing, because they reproduce and surface the emotions, the way the original did.

3. **Generate:** Memorize, put your whole body, heart and soul and become the script. This is a creative exercise. This is what actors in a theatre or a movie do. When we watch a good movie, we don't think of the beauty of the script, nor do we think of the actors. But what we see are characters in the story. This happens because the characters just generate and become the roles they play.

To get to the extent of generating your script, you should have two beliefs:

First: You must believe that have put in the best in your script – that it goes beyond facts and details and tells a story that is close to your heart.

Second: You must believe that you are doing the most important thing of your life and want to do it at your best; you are absolutely willing to invest whatever time and efforts that it may take to make it happen.

If you don't hold these beliefs, then don't memorize your talk. You can just jot down points and have the broad flow in mind, or you may use prompt cards to quickly take a look whenever you need during the delivery.

How do you generate your talk?

This is what the right way of rehearsal is meant to do for you. As you rehearse, take care of the following aspects and keep improving them until you reach the point of rejoicing your talk, like a singer or an actor.

Generating Your Script into a Speech

- **Spontaneity**
- **Mannerisms/ Movements**
- **Appearance**
- **Rhythm**
- **Tackling questions**

Spontaneity

The first draft of the script comes from your writing. The written sentences are usually long and makes sense while reading. But when you read aloud, or, speak it out, you will find that it has a lot of verbiage and lacks the conversational tone. So, the first thing you need to do is to revise your script and make it a more speakable material. You may have to cut down mercilessly all the superfluous material which may look good in reading, but may not be comprehendible to your listeners while delivering it as a talk; break the sentences into short ones; replace high sounding words into simple ones; and finally make the script into a free-flowing talk.

Mannerism

Non-verbal communication like mannerisms, movements, posture and body language form the next part of the rehearsal. When you have fixed up your contents fairly well and you are confident of the flow, you need to work on how and where you are going to stand, whether you will be moving and talking or get fixed to the podium, how you will use your hand gestures etc. At this stage of rehearsal, just go about your speech without getting too concerned about the words you speak.

Appearance

First impressions are strong, and difficult to change. Your audience will tend to judge you from the way you look. By the time you reach the podium, the audience will have already formed an opinion based on their first impressions that come from various signals like your attire, your walking style, your stance, your facial expression etc. Take care of the image you want to create early on, by dressing appropriately, and by rehearsing your stance and style.

Though it is not easy to know the impression you are creating, you can always take the help of your friends or colleagues to get a earnest feedback on these fine points. It is important to consider what you are going to wear in advance, so that you not only look your absolute best for your presentation, but your outfit is appropriate to the occasion and conveys the right image of you to your audience.

Another important and subtler part of your appearance is the emotional expression associated with the contents of your talk. You need to mentally make a note of your emotions as you rehearse your talk and try to resonate emotionally with the contents. When you deliver the actual speech, this practice of emotional articulation will help you enliven your talk.

Rhythm

Rhythm is about the tempo and tonality of your talk. When you have got comfortable with your script, you can focus on the delivery – how effectively you deliver your contents with the weight and significance you desire. Try to get feedback on the pace of your speech, the clarity of your words and diction, the modulations and pitch.

The tone and volume of your voice are crucial to your presentation. Understanding how you can maneuver your voice can be helpful in making your presentation impressive.

Breathing Exercise: Breathe slowly and deeply. This will help improve the flow of blood to the brain, which in turn, will help you think with more clarity and organize your thoughts when speaking in front of an audience. Deep breathing also improves the air flow to your vocal chords, strengthening the throw of your voice and thus reducing nervousness, and helping you gain composure.

Pitching right: It is intonation that often makes a difference in meaning to the same statement. The same statement can mean different things by simply shifting the emphasis from one word to another. If you want your audience to understand your words exactly in your intended sense, then you need to practice the right intonation and pitch with rigor.

Tackling questions

It is important to prepare yourself to answer to the questions that are likely to be thrown by the audience. The key to this is creating your own list of anticipated questions by: a) going through your script and note any unanswered questions that it raises, and (b) by asking your friends or colleagues to raise whatever queries that they have during your rehearsal.

Handling the questions confidently with succinctness and clarity can do well to raise your image as a presenter. Establishing order is important to ensure that no more than one person is talking simultaneously; otherwise the occasion can get out of control. Establish politely that you can only handle one question at a time. Never be drawn into a protracted discussion on any minor point and if it warrants, you may tactfully suggest to the questioner to take the discussion with you offline.

Two ways to get feedback:

One is self feedback. The best way to do this is to watch you deliver the talk in front of a mirror and decipher what to improve upon. You can video-graph and watch it yourself with the above points in mind and keep improving on the things that you feel embarrassed about.

Second is from your trusted group of friends. When you feel ready, you can try rehearsing your speech in front of a small group of good friends or trustable colleagues, who can give you a honest feedback and constructive criticism. Invite them to be frank in pointing out what could be improved and also ask them to suggest how you can make them. Explain to them the context and setting in which you are going to make the presentation, so that they can try to simulate the perspective of real audience.

Rehearsal:

Try to simulate the real scenario to the extent possible during rehearsal and have your close friends and colleagues to have constructive feedback

Checklist

Spontaneity	☐ Have you revised your script to make it flow smoothly and coherently? ☐ Is the opening effective? Is the ending strong? ☐ Do the transitions from one idea to the next work?
Mannerism	☐ Checked on body language and hand gestures? ☐ Taken note of distracting mannerisms/ movements and worked on them? ☐ Became aware of unconscious use of repetitive words or phrases and taken control of them?
Appearance	☐ Are you sporting the right appearance? Are you dressed for the occasion? ☐ How about your posture, gestures and facial expressions- are they in sync with your talk?
Rhythm	☐ How are you managing your Tone and Tenor? Clarity? Are you closing the sentences with right intonations? Are your words clearly spoken? ☐ How is the tempo of the talk? Are there right amount of pauses at right time?
Tackle Qtns	☐ Do you have a list of anticipated questions gathered from your friends and well-thought out responses to them? ☐ Do you feel composed and confident while responding to difficult queries?

14. Closing Strategies

While your 'opening' creates the first impression and gains their attention, it is the 'closing' that can leave a lasting impact with the audience. It is important to end on a high note. It is easy to spoil a good speech with a poor closing that rambles and wanders towards the end. As you become relaxed, you may get reminded of some points missed during your talk or may get new ideas, but don't, by any chance, get tempted to start all over again and give a second speech.

As you begin your concluding note, indicate the transition by proper verbal signpost like *'and finally..'* or *'to putting them together'*, *'let me sum up by recalling ....'* etc.

Cliff-sharp close

A good speech is one that leaves them wanting more. Resorting to a sharp close can be impactful. This style of closing is apt when you have other speakers lined up after you. Here are some strategies for a cliff-end close:

- **Call for action:** You can consider this style of Closing, if you really want to evoke action from your audience.

  Let me give my example: *'which is more exciting of the two- playing the game on the ground or, watching it from gallery? So, if you want to hone your presentation skills, give up the comfort of the gallery and grab the next opportunity to get on to the stage.'*

  The last sentence of the speech by Netaji Subhash Chandra Bose at a rally by Indians in 1944 was *'Give me blood and I promise you freedom'*. That is clear clarion call for action.

- **Quotation:** An appropriate quotation at the end can leave them on a high note. For an inspirational speech, a quote like this could do well *'...and as famously said by Einstein, "there are only two ways to live your life; one is as though nothing is a miracle; the other is as though everything is a miracle'*

- **Question:** Using a well-thought out rhetoric question as the parting line can leave the audience thinking about the talk long after you are done with the talk.

- **Back to the Beginning:** *'We have come to where we began'* is typical of this style. Referring to what you started with provides not only a logical structure, but can even touch the emotional chords of the audience if used effectively.

  One of the finest speeches of US President Barrack Obama during election campaign at Pennsylvania in March 2008 starts with, *'**two hundred and twenty one**'* *years ago*, *in a hall that still stands across the street...'* And the 38 minute speech concludes thus, *'And so many generations have come to realize over the course of* **two hundred and twenty one** *years since the patriots signed the documented Philadelphia, that is where the perfection begins'.*

- **Short film:** A short 2minute-or-less video clip or a specially-made film can pack the essence of the whole talk and make it memorable.

Tapering Close

A gradual close where you can incorporate all the finer elements can work well for a structured presentation. I call this a Tapering Close, where the speech gradually comes to an end on a smooth slope.

In the next chapter, you will find a 'demo' along with the tool for constructing your 'tapering close' that can leave the taste in their memories for long.

15. Last Words

The last words of your presentation have to make a lasting impact, lingering in the minds of your audience for long, lest they become lost words, no sooner than you get off the stage. A well thought out closing impeccably delivered can create this effect.

Here's a *Smart Tool* that takes care of not only the essential elements of 'closing', but also can leave a positive impact among your audience. Go ahead guessing one last time.

Demo

S __ __   U __

Let me put this all together. Now, you have these nine tools that can provide you with a structure for preparing and delivering your talk. You will gain mastery over these tools as you start using them And as you get skilled in using these tools, you can be sure of making a greater and greater impact on your audience.

M__ __ __   t __   A __ __ __ __ __

All you need to do is put these tools into conscious practice at the first opportunity you get. As you become more and more used to the stage, you will find yourself becoming more spontaneous and confident that you don't need these tools anymore; you have already started improvising and evolving your own techniques that suit your style and situation. For that to happen what matters is how quickly you take action on making your presentation using these tools. Now we are providing you with an immediate opportunity to register yourself as a speaker in the 'Smart Pro Forum'. Once you register, you will get an online support on developing your script using these tools. Grab the opportunity NOW.

A__ __   Q __ __ __ __ __ __ __

Surely, some of you are still wondering as to whether you could make it. You need to get those doubts out of the way, right away and go forward. Some of you have some unanswered questions in your mind, you may be looking for more details You can shoot them right away. I am here to clarify all your doubts and reply to your questions.

R__ __ __ __   L__ __ __ __

In the handout, we have provided a list of books and websites that can help you further your learning on this topic. You can also visit our website www.SmartPro-Training.com for online support and assessments. The support team will be more than happy to assist you. You can contact us by phone or mail for any further details.

T__ __ __ __

Thank you all for being here this evening. I heartily thank you for your time and being here for this presentation and am sure you found this of value.

Now take your guess:

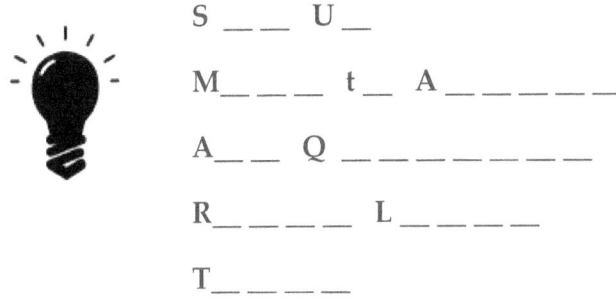

S __ __   U __

M__ __ __   t __   A __ __ __ __ __ __

A__ __   Q __ __ __ __ __ __ __

R__ __ __ __   L __ __ __ __

T__ __ __ __

Concluding Part

As part of preparation, it is vital to work on the closing sentences and rehearse them well so that you make an impact when you deliver.

If you take one more look into the above sample, you will be able to decipher the five components of 'smart closing':

Components of a good 'closing':

Tool

- **Sum up**
- **Move to Action**
- **Allow/ Ask questions**
- **Refer Links**
- **Thank**

Sum up

To indicate that you have come to the concluding part of your presentation, you can use verbal signposts such as *"And now, to sum up briefly before I conclude..."* As said earlier, verbal signposts' are the phrases that signal your transitions in your speech. Indicating that you have come to concluding part, you can get back the attention of audience before you summarize your main points.

It is a good practice to recall what you spelt as your aim in your 'opening' and how you have met with that objective now. Make sure that your summary covers the essence of your presentation. Reinforce those points that you would like the audience remember on the subject matter. A brief summary can be impactful and hence, it is important to summarize your talk in a three or four short and powerful sentences.

Move to Action

'The meaning of communication is the response you get' is one of the postulates of NLP (neuro linguistic programming) . Whether you are giving a motivational talk or persuasive talk, the key test to check whether it has achieved its purpose. It is now the time to ask that crucial question: *Who wants to come along? Who are going to sign up?* This is the litmus test for your effectiveness.

Allow/ Ask Questions

It is a good idea to tell the audience in the introductory part of your talk (remember the 'Treaty') to reserve their questions to the question time. Otherwise, the audience may ask the questions during the presentation which will only interrupt the flow and take away your time for presentation. If time is not a constraint and if you are a seasoned presenter, you may take on the questions as and when they arise rather than pushing to the end.

However, if you are taking the questions at the end you may need to allocate time for this at this stage. You can start the question time with a general question like *'have you got any questions for me?'* Or, *'would anyone like to have more details on this?'*

While responding to questions, it is a good practice to

- appreciate the questioner for good questions
- repeat/ paraphrase the question so that the rest of the audience are clear about the question

- seek clarification from questioner when needed
- to start the answer mainly to the questioner and then turning to all participants with a generalised appraoch
- keep your answer brief and concise and do not get into prolonged discussion
- check back with the questioner whether the question has been answered to his/her satisfaction
- Reinforce the key message while closing the answer.

If there are no questions coming forth from the audience, don't assume that they have no questions to ask. Each of them could be waiting for someone else to open first. You can break the silence by asking a few general, direct questions to encourage them to start the talking. For example, you can ask *'anyone here has a similar experience?'* or, *'Do you get to handle similar issues in work?'* Another way to handle this to be prepared with your own questions like *'some of you may still be wondering ...'* or *'usually I am asked ...'* and then go about answering them. This will ease people into talking.

Refer Links

The listeners may be interested to know more about the subject or may want to connect with you for professional help. You may share the links of internet sites where further information can be obtained. You may refer the books that help in enhancing their knowledge on the subject. You may also take this opportunity to share your contact details like your twitter handle or mail id, indicating your keenness to further the professional relationship.

Thank

Thanking the audience is not just a formal last-but-not-the-least item in the agenda, but a very vital one that needs an earnest expression. Doing it with the right words with the right attitude and humility can leave a lasting impression on the listeners. I have seen some speakers do it with such a heart-touching humility that I am reminded of them whenever I go to the podium. It is said that it is not how much you know that matters, but it is how much you care. Can you heartily share how grateful you feel? Then, you have done it.

Let me give my script for this part to conclude this book. "*I am an ordinary person among the millions. When I walk on the road, no one cares to take a second look at me. Today, you have given me time – you have given me a part of your life – to listen to me and make me feel more than that ordinary person which I always am. The power of the speaker is in the listening of the audience and thank you for allowing me to derive that power today for the last few minutes. I thank you - everyone here listening to me for gifting me with your time – a piece of your life itself.*"

~ Thank You ~

Closing:

Consider how you can structure your 'closing' into this framework.

Checklist

Sum up	☐ Have you summed up the essence of your talk in 3 or 4 statements and how they connect with the purpose? ☐ Does the summary reinforce the key points?
Move to action	☐ Is there an immediate action expected from the audience after your talk? ☐ Have you built into your talk as how to ascertain their stand? ☐ Have you got a support system for follow-up on their affirmations?
Allow/ Ask questions	☐ Have you prepared for the anticipated questions and possible objections? ☐ Have you thought up ways to trigger interaction/ questions in case of no questions?
Refer links	☐ Have you a ready reference of other sources of knowledge relating to the subject? ☐ Have you made a list of reference internet sites, books etc as a handout? ☐ Have you made enough handouts/ brochures/ catalogues for participants)?
Thank	☐ Have you got a way of paying your gratitude in a memorable way?

Presenter's

SMART Tools

- a snapshot

PRESENTER'S SMART TOOLS:
AT A GLANCE

Gather Facts
Subject
Mastery
Audience
Resources
Time

Simple Start
Spark Interest
Motive
Aim
Range
Topic

Rousing Start
Stir up
Mega picture
Assure
Run-up
Treaty

Design Your Talk
Spray Diagram
MoSCoW
Arrange
Resonate
Transitions

Inspire Me (for emotional touch)
Story
Metaphors
Antithesis
Rhetoric qtns.
Triads

Prove It ! (for logical appeal)
Statistics
Merits/demerits
Actual use
Research
Testimonials

Build Your Story
Struggle
Meander
'Aha' moment
Revival
Tomorrow

Try it out
Spontaneity
Movements
Appearance
Rhythm
Tone & tenor

Closing
Sum up
Move to Action
Allow questions
Refer links
Thank

DIY

SMART
Presenter's
WORKBOOK

I. First Facts

Subject	Subject area on which you are required to talk (in less than 12 words)
	When? Where?
Mastery/ Interest (give thought to your differentiators)	Does the subject interest you? Are you passionate about it? Has the subject something to do with your background (your experience/ expertise etc)? Do you have some deep insights/ specialised knowledge on the subject that you want to share? Are you privy to any some unique sources of information on the subject?

Audience	Who? What is common to the group?
	How many (size of audience)?
	From what background?
Resources	Hall/ Auditorium capacity/Seating style?
	Facility to use PPT/ Visuals/Audio systems?
Time	How long is your talk?
	Sequence (if part of a bigger event):
	Time available to you
	Time for Q&A:
Decision	Accept / Decline
Organiser	Name: Contact:

II. Audience analysis

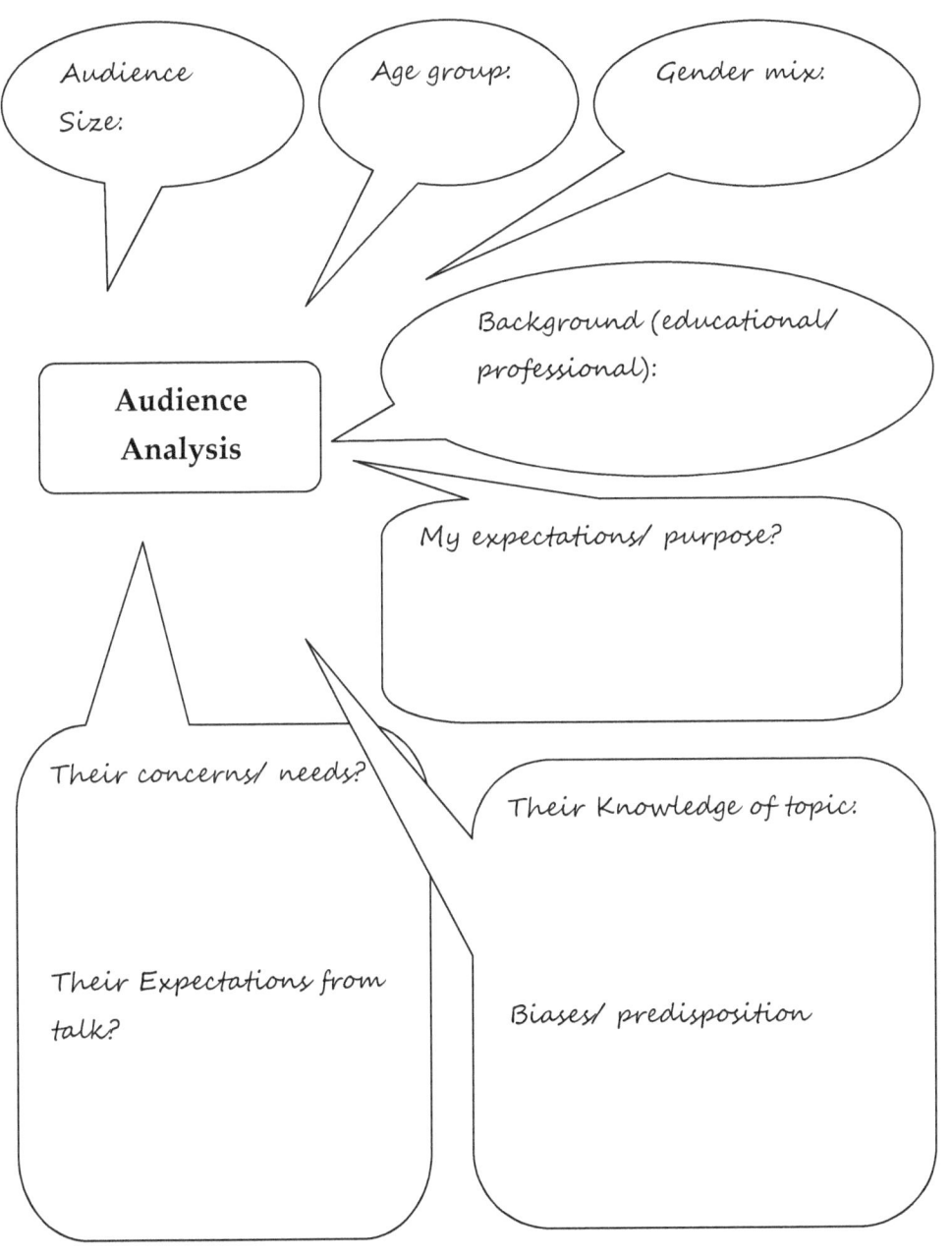

| Key points of Audience Analysis: |
| Unique needs & concerns/ interests & expectations |

| Audience biases and predisposition to the subject |

| Specific Points for the presentation |

III. Purpose

What is the broad purpose of your talk?
☐ To Inform/ to update
☐ To Persuade/ to influence
☐ To motivate/ to inspire
☐ To educate/to instruct/ to explain
☐ To entertain
☐ ....(Ceremonial like Introducing the speaker/ welcome address/ vote of thanks etc)

Purpose: What do you expect from the audience at the end of your talk? How would you know that your talk is effective?

Identify a suitable Title (Appropriate, Brief and Catchy)   Brainstorm for Title ideas

More Title Ideas:

Finalised TITLE of your Talk

Timelines for preparation:

o Gathering ideas:	
o Main structure:	
o Full script with Visuals/ Handouts etc:	
o Rehearsals and Fine-tuning:	
o Ready by:	

Presentation Aids (to be carried with you)

- ☐ Visuals (Laptop/USB drive (PPT)/ Flipchart etc)
- ☐ Handouts / Brochures/ Business Cards
- ☐ Props, if any
- ☐ Presentation Script/ Outline/ Cue cards
- ☐ ....
- ☐ ....

IV.   Gathering Ideas

Put your ideas as they come in a spray diagram to gather your initial thoughts on the subject:

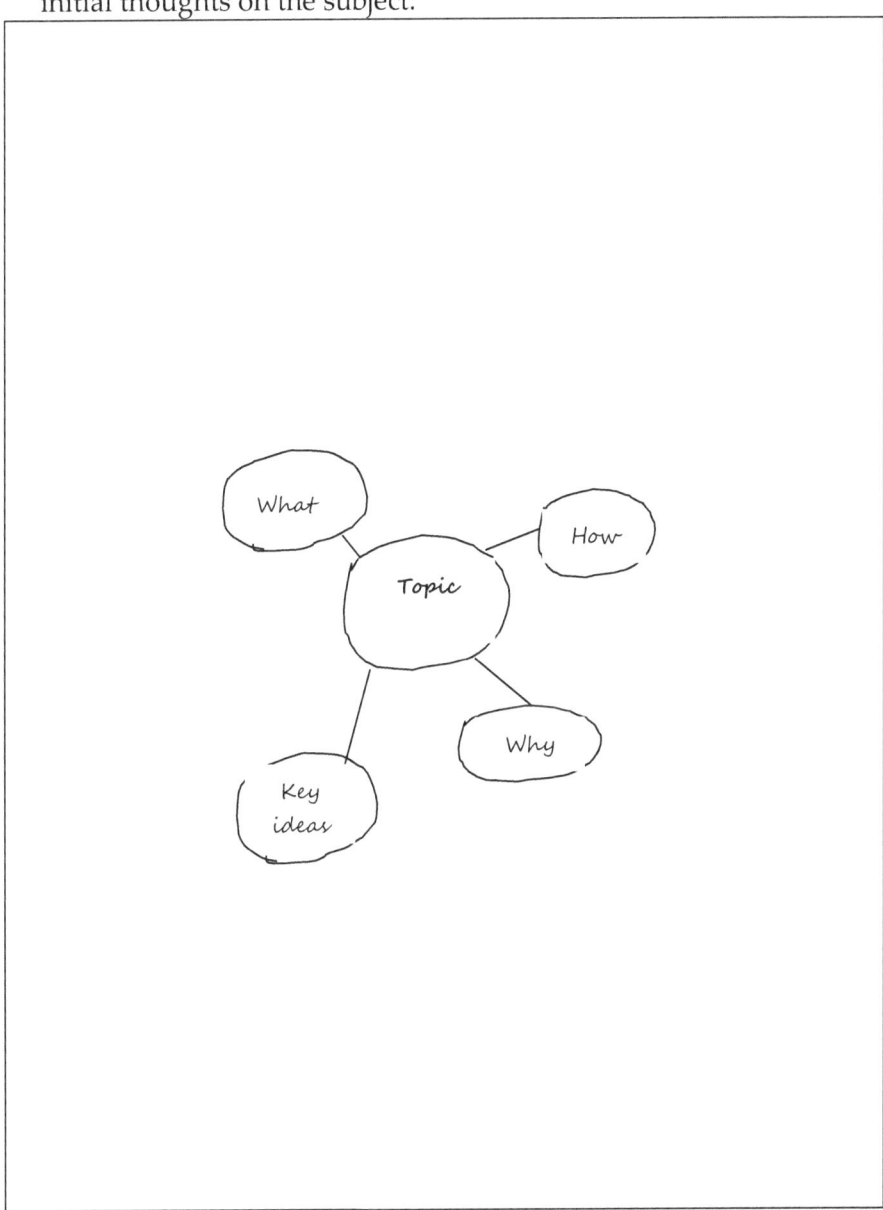

"The audience are likely to remember only three things from your presentation or speech"

— *Stephen Keague*

V. Main Points for Focus

(From your spray diagram, cull out a maximum of 5 Main points for building further)

1..

2. ....

3. ....

4. ....

5. ....

Likely Sources of information for gathering more details

....

. ...

. ...

. ...

. ...

VI.   Building on Main Points

Main Point 1
Support ideas
Visual aid
Transition

Main Point 2
Supporting ideas
Visual aid
Transition

Main Point 3
Supporting ideas
Visual aid
Transition

Main Point 4
Supporting ideas
Visual aid
Transition

"Words have incredible power.
They can make people's hearts
soar,
or they can make people's hearts
sore."

-Dr. Mardy Grothe

VII. Evidential Support

Statistics/ Research findings:

Examples /Illustrations:

Possibility of Demo:

Testimony/ Referrals/ Certificates:

Any other evidence:

VIII. Resonance

Stories/ Anecdotes:
Metaphors/ Analogies
Antithesis/ Rhetoric questions/Triads
Humour:
Any other ornament:

IX.Opening

Formal greeting/ Opening statement / Building rapport
Points for opening (Topic/ benefit/ expectations/ snapshot etc)
State duration / Finish time State the participation/ question time
Transition:

X. Closing

Quick summary:

Call to Action:

Q&A

References/ Links for further learning:

Closing words/ Quote/ Thank:

XI. Rehearsal

Identifying the areas to improve:
Give your frank feedback to the Presenter on the following aspects of the presentation by ticking in the column that best describe your thought on that aspect. If you can qualify your rating with specific suggestions for improvement.

Points for Feedback	Improve it	Just OK	Impressive	Comments
Organising of Content: 1. Is it logical & easy to follow? 2. Does 'Opening' stimulate interest? 3. Is the content and approach interesting and engaging? 3. Are examples, statistics, stories etc, appropriate and interesting? 4. Are transitions clear & signposted? 5. Is it well within time? 6. Does 'closing' leave an impact?				
Delivery: Flow, Pace & Energy: 1. Is it fluent and in conversational tone? 2. Presenter's energy and enthusiasm? 3. Pace of delivery- well-paced? (too fast or slow)				
Gesture/ Eye Contact/ Body language/ Movements: 1. Spreading eye contact? 2. Posture – confident and upright? 3. Use of hand gestures				

4. Movements: gentle or fidgety?				
Points for Feedback	Improve it	Just OK	Impressive	Comments
Auditory Quality: 1. Modulation of voice and tone? 2. Clarity of words and diction?				
Visual: 1. Are the visuals used in right amount? 2. Are they easy to read?				
Handling Questions: 1. Ability to respond confidently? 2. Tact in handling tough questions?				
Points for improvement:				

~ Onward Note ~

Six years back, when I was working on the design of a training course titled 'Smart Manager' for middle level managers, a thought came to me, 'why not use the word smart as an acronym for some of the simple steps involved in preparing and delivering presentations?' And I went about experimenting to develop a few smart tools. When I delivered the course for the first time, not only the participants applied the tool with ease, but brainstorming the tools with the participants helped me in refining some of the words and terms. That enthused me to work on further and build a 'Smart Pro Series' of training which is now shaping up into a book series.

May your SMART Saga continue...

The tools I used for writing the manuscript of this book is a recent version of MSWord on my laptop. Had I written this book some thirty years back, the tools I would have had were pen and paper or at best WordStar, the very early version of MSWord that we use at ease today. See how far we have come.

As we gain skills at using the tools, an incidental thing that happens is the evolution of the tool itself. As you read and apply, it is possible that you come across an idea that sounds better than the original. It would be great, if you want to share such thoughts or ideas that can contribute to bettering the tool. You can get in touch with at delyceum@gmail.com

Stay Smart – Stand Apart

Bharath
Feb 28, 2016

S.M.A.R.T. Pro
Training for
Professional Excellence

SMART Pro *Training Series provides a wholesome training for all-round development of Professionals towards Personal Mastery and Professional Excellence:*

⊕ *SMART Presenter:*
  Stand & Deliver (sans PPT)
⊕ *SMART ScoreCard:*
  Self Improvement: Six Sigma way
⊕ *Career SMART:*
  Roadmap For A Head-start Career
⊕ *Professional's Toolkit:*
  Smart Tools for Thinking & Action
⊕ *Stay Smart- Stand Apart:*
  In Pursuit of Personal Brand

~~~~~~~~

For details of **SMART Pro** training, please logon to:
www.smartpro-training.com
or contact: delyceum@gmail.com
~~~~~~~~~~~~~~~~~~~~~~~

Who is a **S.M.A.R.T. Trainer**?

One who provides learning inputs in

Small Chunks and in

Memorable ways with

Application
        opportunities,

Reinforcement &
        Recognition and

Testing grounds &
        Trust Groups

Become a certified **SMART Pro** Trainer

Take-aways for Certified **SMART Pro** Trainers:

✓ Licence to conduct **SMART Pro** Series of Training
✓ Leader Guide
✓ Participant workbook
✓ PPT Slide Deck
✓ Class Graffiti
✓ Course Promo Brochures
✓ ThinkNote: Booklet of SMART Tools